Nicholas Patrick Wiseman

Points of contact between science and art;

A lecture delivered at the Royal Institution, January 30, 1863

Nicholas Patrick Wiseman

Points of contact between science and art;
A lecture delivered at the Royal Institution, January 30, 1863

ISBN/EAN: 9783337764029

Printed in Europe, USA, Canada, Australia, Japan

Cover: Foto ©ninafisch / pixelio.de

More available books at **www.hansebooks.com**

POINTS OF CONTACT

BETWEEN

SCIENCE AND ART.

BY HIS EMINENCE

CARDINAL WISEMAN.

A LECTURE DELIVERED AT THE ROYAL INSTITUTION,
JANUARY 30, 1863.

LONDON:
HURST AND BLACKETT, PUBLISHERS,
SUCCESSORS TO HENRY COLBURN,
13, GREAT MARLBOROUGH STREET.
1863.

The right of Translation is reserved.

LONDON:
PRINTED BY MACDONALD AND TUGWELL,
BLENHEIM HOUSE, OXFORD STREET.

PREFACE.

In preparing the short-hand notes of the following Lecture for the press, the Author has introduced one or two topics which want of time obliged him to omit, and to expand others which the same reason led him to compress beyond his wishes.

He cannot neglect this opportunity of expressing his thanks to his numerous audience, for the kindness of their reception of him, and the indulgence of their protracted attention to his words.

London, February, 1863.

I. PAINTING . .	PAGE	11
II. SCULPTURE . .	,,	40
III. ARCHITECTURE	,,	62

POINTS OF CONTACT

BETWEEN

SCIENCE AND ART.

THERE is an anecdote of Hannibal with which I am sure every one here is well acquainted. When an exile at a foreign court, he was invited, as you have been this evening, to attend a lecture. He listened to it attentively; but when asked at its close, by one of the admiring audience, what he thought of the performance, with characteristic bluntness he replied, "That it had been his lot in the course of his life to meet with many old dotards, but never with one who so fully deserved that title, as the man who had just dared to discourse upon the art of war, in the presence of Hannibal."

I only fear that you will not wait until the conclusion of my address, to pronounce the same judgment on my presumption; especially as mine is, I fear, a double transgression. I am venturing to address, on the subject of Science, an assembly of men whose reputation for its advancement, or for its cultivation, may be said to pervade the whole of the civilized world. But, in addition to this, I have had the hardihood to announce that I would speak upon Art, in the presence of those who, if their fame has not extended so far—because paintings and marbles are not so portable or communicable as books—at least in their own country can claim preeminence, and stand at the very summit of their most honourable profession.

I fear, therefore, that perhaps you will not wait for the termination of my lecture to form your judgment; I fear you have formed it already—only the kind greetings which I have just now received from you make me hope, that there will be still room for indulgence.

Let me disarm any severer judgment by acknowledging at the onset, that I cannot flatter myself, that any man of science will go away this evening, bearing with him the slightest addition to his scientific knowledge. Neither dare I hope that any artist will receive the slightest instruction, or a new impression, from anything that I can say; and therefore I will throw myself at once upon the kindness of those who I hope form no small portion of my audience—who, like myself, are glad, from time to time, to escape from more engrossing and more systematic pursuits, to spend an hour or two in the company of those two fascinating sisters—Art and Science; and who will feel that they have not mis-spent their time, if they have passed an hour in rational and perhaps not uninstructive recreation

As a preliminary, let me observe that, in speaking of Science and Art, I wish to extend the meaning of one of these words to the utmost, and to restrict that of the other. By Science I wish to understand whatever knowledge has come to man as the result of investigation, by thought, calculation, and experiment—whether the word be referred to the more abstruse and abstract, or to the more practical, exercise of the power of observation; whether these results belong to what may be called the highest range and class of Science, or to what may move in a lower and secondary plane. By Art, on the other hand, I wish not to understand the Arts of Life, as they are called, or the Practical Arts, but the Fine Arts; and even those restricted to the Arts of Design—to those which approach our intellect and our feelings through the eye, not including those which make their way, like Poetry or Music, through another organ. *

The union which I have proposed to establish between the two is one so obvious, that I have feared I may have selected a very commonplace subject in thus joining the two together—" The points of contact between Science and Art." In familiar discourse we can hardly speak

* I need hardly allude to the repeated efforts made, ever since Newton's time, to establish relations between music and colours; that is, between spaces in the musical scale, and those in the prismatic colours. A magnificent work, purporting to give a perfectly demonstrated view of these analogies, with two atlases of coloured plates, two hundred in number, has been announced in France, under the title of " Du Vrai, du Beau, et de l'Utile," or " Harmonies Comparées." An introductory and detailed *Mémoire* of it was submitted to the Scientific Congress at Bordeaux in 1861, and was published there the same year. It was favourably received. I believe the parts which were to follow have not appeared. The author, whose name does not anywhere appear, but, I understand, is F. Duland, promises practical applications of his results to other sciences.

of the one without the other; they seem to go necessarily hand-in-hand. But I hope it may be seen that there are points in which they have not yet come sufficiently into contact, and which deserve a closer connection; so that it should be our endeavour, if possible, to knit still more straitly this natural union.

If we look around us in this great city, we see how indispensable it is considered, that the cultivation of the two should be carried on in common.

Our three great Museums, to which I need not more particularly allude, are all of them of a mixed character; so that the objects of Science, in its various branches, are almost always to be found blended or associated with objects of Art.

If, however, speaking not of places, but of persons, I had to choose, from ancient times, the "representative man" of this union, it would be the great artist Leonardo da Vinci, so well known as a consummate painter, comparatively less acknowledged as one of those great men connected with the chain of Science, who kept patiently and sagaciously adding link to link, until it has gained its present perfection. Leonardo da Vinci finds his place both in the history* and in the philosophy† of the Inductive Sciences; and in the latter, among "the practical reformers of Science," a high character to be given by such a competent judge as the author of those works, to one whose merits are chiefly known by the productions of his pencil. In fact, he left thirteen volumes of scientific sketches, of diagrams and of mechanism, chiefly connected with hydraulics; which unfortunately have been removed from the place where he left them, by the vicissitudes of modern times, and are to be found now chiefly in Paris.‡

But we need not go back so far as three centuries, to fix upon one in whom has been concentrated this twofold feeling; and that so equally and impartially in his blending affections, that we might say he never saw Art without Science, never looked at Science without seeing Art; and who considered both as the great moving powers by which civilisation and progress were

* Whewell's "History of the Inductive Sciences," vol. ii., p. 122.
† "Philosophy of the Inductive Sciences," vol. ii., p. 368.
‡ The descriptions attached to the drawings often, if not always, require to be read in a mirror, as they are written reversed.

to be advanced in this, his adopted country. You will easily understand that I allude to that Prince so lately taken from us, who for many years studied to the utmost the means of prosperity for England, and became convinced that none was more important than to bring together, as far as possible, these two great manifestations of intellectual cultivation and of social refinement.

I cannot help, at the opening of this discourse, alluding to the care with which he seized every opportunity of inculcating the necessity of cultivating the two harmoniously, and inseparably, yet independently. In his public speeches the Prince Consort alluded constantly to this idea; but perhaps on no occasion more markedly than a few years ago, on laying the first stone of an Institute—of "the Birmingham and Midland Institute"—intended for the cultivation of both Science and Art.

After alluding to this happy alliance, he spoke as follows:—

"You will thus have conferred an inestimable boon on your country; and in a short time have the satisfaction of witnessing the beneficial results upon our material powers of production.

Other parts of the country will, I doubt not, emulate your example; and I live in hope that all these Institutions will some day find a central point of union."*

These words, and others like them, were the germ, sorrowful but glorious, from which has sprung the great idea of erecting, as his memorial, a noble hall of combined Science and Art; in which the two can meet in friendship, and mutually support, assist, and grace each other.

If a national monument should permanently record the characteristic thought of him to whom it is erected; and if the memorial would be still grander, if it can actually carry out that thought, and render it enduringly efficacious—surely the embodying of the Prince's desire and suggestion, in such a monument as has been proposed, will be, without exception, the most appropriate and useful mausoleum that has yet been ever seen.

Hence it seems wise and natural, that the Committee appointed by the Crown to report on this subject, should have suggested the carrying

---

* "Speeches and Addresses," p. 171. See also pp. 164-167, and 112. At the inauguration of the Horticultural Gardens, similar expressions are said to have been used; but the discourse is not published in this volume.

out of the Prince's idea, as the most appropriate manner of publicly honouring his memory.*

But the high sanction of this proposal is so striking, and so authoritative, that you will allow me to detain you one moment, by reading a few words from it:—"Knowing the importance attached by the Prince to the establishment of one central institution, for the promotion of artistic and scientific education." And again, "The Queen knows how constantly he regretted, that much of the good attending many of the institutions founded for the advancement of Science and Art was lost by their isolation and want of connection with each other."† I have no right to constitute myself the mouthpiece of an Association which stands so deservedly high among our national institutions, as that at whose desire I have the honour to address you, and which has better ways undoubtedly of making itself heard throughout the country; but may I be allowed, as a representative of the many to whom I have

---

* See the letter of the Committee of Architects, to Sir C. Eastlake, on this proposal, June 5, 1862.

† Col. Grey's letter, July 18, approving of this scheme; designs for which have been prepared by several eminent architects.

alluded, as mere lovers of Science and Art, and who will not refuse the voice of one of themselves, to express my conviction, that there will be, and must be, a universal response to words so spoken. And as the thought did not occur to me, that the topic which I had chosen for my lecture bore the remotest analogy to this higher subject of deliberation, till long after I had decided upon it, I have, I own, received encouragement from this coincidence. For the very study of my theme, and my reflection on it, have naturally led me to conclude, that it would be impossible to erect a more fitting and splendid monument than has been proposed, to one whose history presents this rare, if not singular, feature; that the reverence and affection for the memory of his many noble qualities and gracious gifts seem to become more and more vivid, in proportion as we recede from the sorrowful period at which these began to be only a memory.

In treating my subject I will simply take the Arts of Design in the order in which they are commonly enumerated. I will begin with Painting; then, as time may permit, I will try to say something concerning Sculpture and Architecture.

I.—PAINTING.

What is the most obvious point of contact between the art of Painting and practical Science? I know what everybody will answer. "Of course," it has been repeated to me by many persons to whom I have spoken on the subject, "it is in the science of Perspective." This is at first sight a barren subject, but I think it is capable of interesting illustration. Every one, though the term is not very old, now fortunately knows what is meant by Perspective. It signifies the art of representing, on a flat surface, objects which are supposed to be in different planes, or at varying distances, so as to give them, by the gradation of proportions and of colour, the appearance to the eye which they would have if they were real substantial objects.

This science, simple as it appears, and familiar as it is to us, is by no means very old; yet, how it began, in what way it sprang up, is certainly a problem. There is no question that

Art, when last revived, seized more or less at once practically upon the principles by which the science is ruled; and that the great painters, having a quickness and facility in catching objects as they appear to the eye, gave them in their works that same effect. But as a science diffused, and well known, it was a long time before the rules of Perspective can be said to have pervaded the whole of Art.

It may be useful to observe, that accurate Perspective requires the combination of two elements—the one scientific, the other artistic. The scientific consists of a disposition of the objects in their proper distances and ratios, geometrically determined; and the artistic, or aerial perspective, in their receiving the gradation and evanescence of tone, which distance furnishes in real nature.

Attention to both these points appears very early, and simultaneously, in two distant countries; by one of those mysterious sympathies, which often strike us in the history of Art;—in Belgium and Italy, in the schools of Van Eyck and of Giotto.

The two brothers Van Eyck—Hubert, who died in 1426, and John, who died in 1446,—

who painted together, were clearly masters of perspective in both its branches. Speaking of one of their paintings, Lord Lindsay observes, that " the architecture is particularly well painted, and Van Eyck here appears as the forerunner of Neefs and Steenwich;"* he might have added, of our own Roberts.

Again, he writes of John, that "it is perhaps for his improvements in perspective, lineal and aerial, that he deserves our warmest gratitude: the former had indeed long been studied in the South, but for the latter we are almost exclusively beholden to him." †

It would, indeed, have been strange if Florence had been behind Bruges in the discovery of such an essential condition of good painting. Before the time of Giotto, through the long period of Byzantine Art in fresco and mosaic, it had remained unknown; and we trace the efforts made to attain it which imperfect Art, in the hands of struggling genius, prompted. But in the school, and the successors of that reviver of true Art, there is evidence that not mere personal observa-

* " Sketches of the History of Christian Art," vol. iii., p. 299.
† Ibid, p. 304.

tion and individual cleverness enabled some gifted artists to seize this necessary ingredient of pictorial Art, but that it was reduced to principles, formed into precepts, and taught to scholars. "The Giotteschi, especially Giusto of Padua, had taken the first steps in linear perspective; and Uccello, Pietro della Francesca, Bramantino, Alberti, and other Italian artists, advanced it greatly, both by precept and example, towards the middle of the fifteenth century."*

Of these perhaps Pietro della Francesca deserves special notice. He died in 1482, at the advanced age of eighty-four, and was in every respect a great artist, not only on account of his own works, but on account also of the great influence which he exercised upon Art. For there is evidence that he not only understood and practised perspective with great accuracy, as Vasari records of him, and his own paintings testify, but he reduced its principles to writing in three books, said still to exist.† This is certain, that from his time dates that accuracy in drawing

---

* Ibid.

† See the preface to the splendid work (fol., with atlas) by Cav. Annibale Angelini, "Trattato teorico pratico di Prospettiva," Rome. 1861, p. xx.

temples, triumphal arches, and other edifices which we see in the works of Luca Signorelli, Baldassare Peruzzi, Perugino, and others. It is not a slight coincidence, but a suggestive fact, that, about twenty years before his death, he should have been a guest of Giovanni Santi, Raffaele's father, where he may perhaps have sown the seeds of the son's perfection.

Certain it is, that before the literature of perspective commences, that prince of artists, as in his School of Athens, or his *Incendio del Borgo*, and his rival Michelangelo, had shown themselves consummate in the application of perspective to Art.*

Here begins the history of Scientific Perspective; that is, the first true contact of Science with the art of Painting; when the anticipations of Art were verified by Science, and reduced to unvarying rule.† As we have seen, in the first practical

* Ib., p. xiii. The ceiling of the Sixtine Chapel is a triumphant evidence of Buonarotti's skill in perspective, and in the kindred power of foreshortening, so totally unknown before Giotto.

† The history of the literature of perspective will be found most completely sketched and analysed in a series of "Notes on Perspective," by Mr. A. De Morgan, in the *Athenæum*, from October to November, 1861. To these articles I am much indebted for what follows.

exercise of the science of perspective, a remarkable coincidence between its discoveries in northern and southern Europe, the same singular uniformity is to be found, in this next step, its public, and more accurate explanation. In the first instance, Art forestalled Science in two distant countries at the same time; in the second, Science overtook Art almost in the same manner. Leonardo da Vinci, whom I have already described as representing to us the union of Science and Art, who died in 1519, and Albert Dürer, whose death occurred in Nürnberg, in 1528, a mathematician as well as painter, were here the worthy agents in this great advancement of Art. Both indeed united in themselves the two qualifications requisite for that purpose, proficiency in Science as in Art. Notwithstanding the success which practically followed the example and precepts of these great artists, we are told that "the sixteenth century may be described as the day of a very few rules, and laborious application guided by natural sagacity."*

It was not till 1608 that the first satisfactory treatise on this subject was published by Guido Ubaldo.

* *Athenæum*, Oct. 26, p. 541.

In 1642, F. Dubreuil edited his *Prospectiva Practica*, well-known to artists under the title of the Jesuit's Perspective.

Finally, it was only in 1731 that the mathematical theory of perspective was demonstrated by Brook Taylor.*

Slowly, therefore, and patiently, did Science follow the more rapid steps of Art, to complete, to enlarge, to perfect, and to perpetuate its almost instinctive discoveries. It has been well said by Mr. de Morgan, that " the first-class draughtsman managed, in one way or another, to do all that could be done; the difference between one

---

* There was a period of retrogression in every department of Art, and, of course, in the right use of perspective. It was, when abuse in its application took place of its legitimate use, when display of perspective became the sole aim of the artist, when it ceased to be an accessory, but the entire subject of his picture. This does not, of course, apply to the representation of interior architecture, with its beautiful effects of light and shade; but to the attempt to deceive, by trying to make columns appear straight upon arched ceilings, or domes circular on flat surfaces. The chief in these *tours de force* is Andrea Pozzo (1695), whose vault in the church of St. Ignatius in Rome, and domes there, and at Frascati, are certainly wonderful, but pedantic and unpictorial. The rules for executing these extravagances will be found in the splendid edition of his works in two volumes, folio, Rome—the *first* in 1762, the *second* in 1758.

period and another lies in the facility of the mode of doing it." That is to say, as soon as Science came to bring its resources to bear on Art, it demonstrated certain principles, which came thereby to be so fixed and proved, that it was impossible ever afterwards to allow deviation from them. But, whenever Science has thus acted in a matter of practical importance, the next step is to convert its theorems into practical rules, which are accepted, for all necessary and useful purposes, without further proof. We have an illustration in arithmetic: we teach thousands and tens of thousands of children to perform complicated operations in what was formerly considered one of the great sciences, without the least understanding why they should so divide, or so multiply, or so deal with fractions, or solve equations; but simply because they have a plain rule taught them, which they are not the least conscious has been the subject of strict and accurate mathematical demonstration. The consequence is, that you can teach and tutor, and train a whole nation to anything you like, if you can once get it to accept the formulas proved and demonstrated by science, as simple admitted truths and rules of practice.

Let us now see the corresponding effect here. From the moment that perspective was reduced to certain and scientific principles, and was so accepted by Art, it became almost impossible to deviate from them; they were soon popularized; they were adopted as an essential part of artistic education, reduced to rules easily learnt and applied; so that no one would dare now to produce what would have passed muster a few centuries ago, by painting even a signboard out of perspective. It would be impossible, without its appearing the very height of the ridiculous, to reproduce Hogarth's well-known illustration of want of perspective in one of his engravings. We have got thus far, then, in educating the public eye to Art.

In order to explain what I mean by this expression, permit me to make a little digression; because I think I can make it understood from another art. Let me take you back to the year 1733, to Oxford, when, at a commemoration, Handel made his appearance, to perform his oratorio of "Esther." We have the record of what happened from one who was in the city at the time. I cannot read some of the expressions, but he says that "one Handel, a foreigner," came; and tells us of "the players being denied by the Vice-Chancellor coming to Oxford, and that very rightly, though they might as well have been here, as Handel and (his — crew) a great many fiddlers." "His book," he adds, "worth one penny, he sells for a shilling." In the description of that first performance of "Esther," "fiddling" is the most honourable term that is applied to it.* Then soon afterwards you have him in London; and Horace Walpole, whom we are accustomed to look upon as a man of the most refined taste in all that relates to Art, speaks of him with the utmost contempt, even scorning and ridiculing his "Hallelujahs," as he calls them; and we are told that "the ladies invented those balls and tea-parties which were so fatal to the performances of Handel.... nay, even got up a puppet-show, by a mimic of the lowest class, in opposition to the oratorios of Handel."† Now, let us imagine that great composer, after one of these heavy rebuffs, meditating in his own mind upon what he really felt his place

---

* Quoted from "Hearn's Memoirs," by Victor Schoelcher, in his "Life of Handel." 1857. P. 157.
† Ib.. 293.

ought to be; and we can imagine him, as those magnificent and heavenly harmonies floated through his mind and his imagination, shedding tears of bitterness, at the idea that the world was not worthy of him, and that he should be so persecuted and vilipended. But, whatever may have been his own splendid thoughts upon the way in which, if he could have had his will, he would have wished himself and others to hear his music, he may, perhaps, have never reached that which has been really attained. His friend Pope—one of the few he had—represents a meeting between "La Mancha's knight and a dramatic author," who, after having shown him how completely his composition was in accordance with all Aristotelian precepts, expresses regret that there is one scene which he is sorry to say he must omit, because it would violate those rules. "And what is that?" "Why, a battle with its knights and squires must be cut out, because it would be impracticable." "What!" exclaims the knight-errant, "cut out the battle? No, knights and squires all must come on."

The poor poet remonstrates—

"So vast a throng the stage could ne'er contain."
"Then build a new, or act it on a plain,"

responds the undaunted Don Quixote.* We naturally consider such a proposal as a fanciful exaggeration of artistic enthusiasm. But what if Handel had imagined that this would one day be the history of his music? Why, he would have been right. That a stage such as the world had never before seen should be erected, in a vast palace of crystal, especially to exhibit and commemorate his musical genius—that there would be as many crowded upon it as would have peopled a plain; and if we add the vast audience—the tens of thousands that were there, that no plain in the world could have assembled so many persons as would come to do him honour, and to listen rapturously to his performances—to have dreamt of such a retribution, would have been beyond his powerful fancy; yet if he had, his would have been a prophetic dream.

Now, the public ear has been trained to the perception and to the relish of the most sublime music perhaps ever composed; and that in the

* Essay on Criticism.

course of these hundred and thirty years. But that is far below truth. Who are those that crowd that gigantic platform to perform this music? Are they professional musicians, selected from two or three cathedral choirs? Or, are they members of some particular philharmonic societies, composed of ladies and gentlemen, as it used to be formerly, who gave the public a treat in listening to the "Messiah?" No; they are the men and the women taken from the looms, and from behind the mules of Manchester and Bolton, and other manufacturing cities; they are the choral societies of villages of Lancashire or Yorkshire, or of other counties, and in the neighbourhood of the Metropolis. And these men and women, who had never met before, have been brought together in London; and the scores of that most difficult music have been put into their heads, as any one will remember who has been present, even at their first rehearsals; and not only have these thousands of voices united for the first time in singing it with magnificent precision, but they have been enabled to relish, and to give expression to, every variety of itst ones, from the flowing undulations of a thanksgiving hymn, to the crash of the hailstone chorus,—all under the command of one single baton, in the hand of one who has fully atoned for the wrongs that his countrymen committed during his life, against that matchless composer.

We have been able, therefore, completely to educate the public *ear*, and, I may say, almost the public voice, to the proper appreciation of the sublimest in the Art of Music. Can we do the same for Painting? Why not? Look at the step already made in what I before described. It hardly seems credible that nations can have existed with an Art of their own, exercising it under the highest patronage for hundreds, nay, thousands of years, and never have attained the slightest perception, by their eye, of this to us elementary science. I say nothing of the Greeks and Romans. We know very little of their Art, beyond their matchless power of delineating the human form. We have none of their great paintings at all remaining. There exist only a few fragments, and they are chiefly decorative. Pompeii itself gives us little clue to the knowledge of the ancients in this part of Pictorial Art; the excuse given for defects there, is, that only an inferior class of artists worked at the arabesque ornaments found. But this is exactly the proof required, that perspective had not been reduced to such simple and obvious rules, as to have been attainable by every artist. The only passages which have been brought from Vitruvius and Pliny to establish the knowledge of the science of perspective by the ancients, relate exclusively to the producing of scenic effects. We may, therefore, reasonably conclude, that—as at the last revival of Art—first-rate artists, the great painters, had an eye which would not allow them to violate the principal rules of perspective; but we have no evidence that it was a popular, universally-practised portion of Art.

Of Assyrian art we have many monuments in our Museums, extending over a period of several centuries; and what an utter neglect or ignorance there is in them of everything that relates to distance! Men are fighting in the skies; boats are swimming through the depths of the current; the city is represented as a flat surface; and its walls are out of all proportion with the figures, and the figures with them. In fact, it is quite clear, as far as we can judge from their monuments, that they had no rules by which to regulate the disposition of their figures, so as to give any idea of receding spaces.

The Egyptians clearly had the same ignorance: for in their paintings there is no attempt at representing any gradation of distance in objects or in figures. Hundreds of people are crowded into the same scene—all exactly alike, and all at the same distance apparently, with the same proportions and the same movements. The only difference there is in size is on the sort of principle which we remember in "Jack, the Giant-killer"—the king is a giant, a man of enormous proportions, who holds a dozen or more of pigmy kings by the hair, and is going to strike off their heads at one blow.

The Chinese, likewise, with such beautiful colours, and with such taste in the delicate delineation of natural objects—flowers, insects, or birds, yet, when they come to paint any composition—even a hand-screen—cannot put the lines of the different parts of the building conformably to the laws of perspective.*

---

* In Chinese paintings, even where perspective skill is shown in the principal scene, the foreground will be found in much reduced proportions—in miniature, in fact; and the background figures will be seen diminished beyond all ratio.

When, therefore, we find that whole nations may have lived for ages, painting in royal palaces and majestic temples, with no knowledge whatever of perspective, and without arriving at a perception of its absence—it is not a trifle to have done what we have, and to have made perspective now so natural, and so universally felt, that it is impossible any longer to tolerate the violation of its laws. This is one great step forward in national artistic education, due to the contact between Science and Art.*

Now comes the question, Can we go further still? And the answer will perhaps result from remarks which I shall have occasion to make later. But here let me observe, that in one branch of Pictorial Art we have, I think, succeeded in educating the public eye and the public mind; and you may, perhaps, be inclined to smile if I attribute even that progress some-

---

The fact is, that importance, not distance, regulates the pictorial proportions. And this, no doubt, meets the demands of the Chinese eye, or rather idea, in Art.

* In referring, as one naturally does, to this country, it is not meant to insinuate, that similar progress has not been made elsewhere. Every country, which possesses an art, has partaken of the improvements that have taken rise in every other.

what to mechanical and scientific proficiency. We have done much to inspire the people of this country, in every class, with a perception of the beautiful in nature—the love of landscape, of sea and land. Some years ago, I took the liberty of stating in a lecture which I published, that we could find no traces of the real love of natural beauty among the classical poets—none that could bear comparison with what pervades our modern bards. I was glad afterwards to find the learned illustrator of Homer in our time, and the most eloquent writer on Art, both agree in the same opinion.* This may appear singular, but, in fact, as far as we can judge, that branch of Art which confines itself to the representation of nature, was little known or

* "On the Perception of Natural Beauty, by the Ancients and Moderns," delivered Dec. 10, 1855. Mr. Gladstone, on the whole, acknowledges that Homer had not much eye for landscape beauty ; " Studies on Homer and the Homeric Age," 1858, vol. iii., p. 419, *seq.* He does not give full assent to Mr. Ruskin's sweeping declaration, that "Homer has no trace of feeling for what we call the picturesque." Mod. Painters, p. 4, c. xiii. (1856). Mr. Gladstone, in his chapter on "Colour in Homer," (ib., p. 489,) acknowledges : "I conclude, then, that the organ of colour and its impressions were but partially developed among the Greeks of the heroic age." Surely this is incompatible with the love or appreciation of natural beauty.

appreciated among the ancients. It is comparatively so yet in Italy. I have been surprised to see how little taste or feeling for beautiful natural scenery there is, in a country where it so much abounds.*

What I am about venturing to ask is this—

* Many years ago, when a youthful resident in Italy, I remember being struck with this fact, that scenes, before which foreigners would linger for hours, time after time, would be passed by with indifference by natives possessed of good taste, and even of artistic accomplishments. This often formed the subject of interesting speculation, but not of easy understanding. A natural solution offered itself in the supposition, that the native eye was too much accustomed to natural beauty, especially lit up by such skies as Perugino or Francia delighted in, to lead the mind up to high emotions. This, however, is far from a satisfactory reply to the difficulty. England possesses also a class of charming national scenery, not known in Italy—the calm landscape of river or brook, and tree, with homely adjuncts—which does not habituate us to indifference in reality or on canvas. The beauties of our rivers and their banks, in every part of England, have had full justice done them by Mr. Ruskin, in his "Modern Painters." Must we have recourse to the useful hypothesis of races, and suppose that the Teutonic eye has a keener instinct, and the Teutonic mind a finer relish, for landscape beauty; while the Græco-Italian has corresponding gifts in connection with what is called beauty of form? Certainly the "*paesista*" does not rank in Italy among highest-class artists; nor has the country possessed beyond a very limited number of native landscape painters.

it may seem absurd, perhaps—but why is it that in England we are all so keenly alive to the perception of this beauty in nature? Is it not, in part at least, because where formerly one person moved from his home, ten thousand do now. The railway carries them to every beautiful point of scenery in places which they select on its very account. The sea-shore is crowded, and no place on it so much as where there is a rich variety of rock and wave. The lake scenery in England and in Scotland, the wild coasts of the west of Ireland, the Pyrenees, Switzerland, the Rhine—are all thronged, year by year, with multitudes of pilgrims after the beautiful, from a class wherein formerly there was little or no appreciation of it; and they return, no doubt, with their minds impressed with finer feelings; and gradually those impressions must deepen and widen, until we may hope to find their whole minds richly impregnated with the most wholesome sentiments—with thoughts of a more solemn character than the appreciation and love of mere nature; that admiration being directed to the greatness and power of its Author and Creator.

Whether we shall arrive at training the

popular taste to understand that form of Art which records historical actions, remains yet to be seen. It is certain that if we do wish this Art to be understood and relished, we must provide means for bringing it more within the reach of those whom we desire to instruct.*

We have not done anything like even what foreign nations have, in seconding and directing the public taste. The great modern works of Art which should interest the public are shut up from them. There is little opportunity, even in our largest and most educated cities, of seeing large paintings and great works of Art. The number of artists who can undertake them is necessarily small; but if the demand for that highest Art increases, no doubt plenty of genius will come forth from this country, to be able to satisfy all the wants of artistic progress in every part of the kingdom.

The ancients built porticoes almost on purpose to afford public, yet sheltered, wall-space for

---

* Ten people in England can form a judgment on the merits of a Gothic building, for one who could pronounce accurately on a classical one. This arises from familiarity with good specimens of the one style, ancient and modern, and the want of it, with good models, of the other.

serieses of paintings. Augustus did this, when he rebuilt the old Septa, or voting-pens, in Rome.* At Munich similar opportunity has been afforded for frescoes. Even covered bridges, like that of Lucerne, have served as ground for the exercise of Art. Cloisters and cemeteries have similarly served it; not to speak of chapels, churches, domes and ceilings. In Italy every princely house contains at least one great hall (the *sala*), the vault of which, if not the walls, is often covered with mighty works by the greatest artists.

Of all this we possess nothing; nor are we likely to see these colossal and multiplied works within the easy access of the people. Our very domestic habits would forbid it. Nor can we hope that frescoes in the Houses of Parliament, and their purlieus, will exercise any real influence over the multitudes who even live in London, without ever seeing them.

The Museum at Versailles has been a grand attempt to guide public taste, or rather feeling: for it is to the war-scenes, and their national glory there commemorated, not to the Art

---

* Cicero to Atticus, l. iv.. 16.

which immortalises them, that the national interest is drawn.*

There is no doubt that opportunities corresponding to those which I have enumerated, offer themselves abundantly in those institutions, and the edifices erected for them, which belong more strictly to our country and age. Exchanges, Halls of Commerce, Music and Lecture Halls, Scientific Institutes, even Mansion-houses or Town-halls, would easily furnish porticoes or colonnades, with their walls or vaults, and very large rooms, in which ample spaces would be found for noble pictures, analogous to the object of the building.

But am I not wandering from my subject? What contact is there here between Science and Art? A very important one, on which, however, I can only briefly touch. It is rather of a want of such needed contact that I have to speak; for it relates to colour. Here again Art has run before Science.

* It would not be fair to mention this as the only encouragement given in France to highest Art. Any one who has visited Flandrin's works in the Church of St. Vincent of Paul, in Paris, will see how amply room, scope, and means are provided by French patronage, for pictorial works on a noble scale.

We do not know very much about ancient colours. We know they were very few, and very simple, and a certain account of them has come down to us; but how they were mixed or applied, we know but little. This, however, is certain—that after eighteen hundred years we find mural paintings still fresh, their colours as yet often even vivid—generally without having altogether vanished.

Coming to the first periods of modern Art, we find frescoes out of doors, on the fronts of houses, suffering, no doubt—some of them dreadfully—from damp and weather; but they are still there, and there they promise to remain, at least distinguishable, for a very much longer period. Surely with the accurate knowledge we have of the chemical action of substances, one upon another, with the immense resources also that Chemistry has given us in new and beautiful pigments, with the power of analysing any deleterious qualities, whether in the lime or in other components of the ground on which the paintings have to be executed, there appears no reason, why we should be behind what seems to have been almost left to accident, by those older painters. We know that all the mediæval artists, and those of later schools, mixed their own colours. They employed men, who sometimes, from the low occupation of grinding colours for superior artists, rose to be themselves great masters, by living among the great works, and receiving the kind assistance, of those who had taken them into their studios.

Then, as they painted frescoes in villages, or country houses, for the lowest prices, we cannot doubt that they took their chance as to the qualities and preparation of their *intonaco*, or plaster, from the hands of ordinary masons. A few years ago, in Città della Pième, there was a discovery in the oratory of the Disciplinati, which Pietro Perugino painted, of some original letters, bargaining about the conditions for that beautiful work, which is quite fresh as yet; and some of his colours were supposed to be found walled up with them; but they were no longer distinguishable.[*]

We know that there was nothing particular or recondite about ancient colours. They were

---

[*] This was in 1835. Soon after I saw the letters, which I gave with an account of their discovery, in the *Dublin Review*, July 1839—republished in "Essays on various subjects," vol. iii., 481.

what we should consider common and simple and wholly primitive. But clearly there is something which we as yet want to come up to them; and that must be supplied by Science. Science must come to the aid of Art, and answer the question : " Is there any atmospheric or other chemical, action in this country, which prevents our carrying out in it such public works of Art as exist in other countries?" It is not that we are unable to produce beautiful paintings, but we desire to see something produced—

——" quod et hunc in annum
Vivat, et plures ,"

—something that will go down for centuries, to show the world what Art was with us, in our times.

At first sight, it appears incredible that any amount of atmospheric damp could obliterate, or evaporate, a fresco in a few years, more effectually than the humidity of the soil, percolated by nearly two thousand years' rain, and piled upon, or against, a wall, has done in Pompeii. Yet this is, or threatens to be, the case here. It surely is a point on which Science should come to the rescue of Art, a point of friendly and useful contact.

Now, suppose that, after an earnest examination of this question, it should be decided that fresco painting is, and must be, a failure in our climate ; and that, moreover, all *silicating*, or other external, processes, are illusory, what remains ? There is still one resource left, the most durable and unalterable transcript of the painter's work—Mosaic. So far from fearing damp, it seems to flourish in it. Nowhere has it been better preserved, in defiance of climate, than at Ravenna; not only in the city churches, but in the great church in Classe, or out of the gates, in as damp a situation as can well exist. This subject, however, has been so fully and so learnedly treated by a distinguished living artist, that I will not dwell on it, beyond borrowing a few lines from his Essay.

"Mural painting," says Mr. Digby Wyatt, "must in our climate ever have to contend with elements certain to shorten its ephemeral beauty. . . . . What, then, is left us but those processes, over the most delicate and the boldest pictures produced by which, experience has proved that a thousand years may pass, ' and steal no grace away.'"* I did not say that this was mosaic.

What I desire, however, to call particular attention to is this: Dealing with mosaic, not as an architectural ornamentation, but as a durable and almost eternalizing process of painting—not as a surface of tesselation, but as a glowing, living picture, the chemist must be called in, to assist, or almost to create, the art. First, the mastic, in which the vitrified colour is to be sunk or embedded, must be such as to resist time, damp, and, if on the ground, the tread and stamp of countless feet. Then the gradation of colours must be minute and varied; for every tint of every colour must proceed from its deepest to its most evanescent hue. In the great Vatican studio, the production and progression of new colours, and shades, are entirely in the hands of a chemist, who commands and directs the laboratories and furnaces requisite for the work. And one must inspect "the catalogues," or graduated specimens of colours

* "On Pictorial Mosaic as an Architectural Embellishment." Read at the Royal Institute of British Architects, March 17, 1862.

in the workshop, to believe in the nicety of succession in each series. In all they number upwards of twenty thousand.

If, therefore, we are to persevere in fresco painting, as a monumental art, chemistry must be seriously invoked to lend its almost infallible aid, to secure our great works from speedy decline, and secure them, if not immortality, at least longevity. And if Science declare itself powerless to cope with natural obstacles, and advise us to have recourse to more durable materials, it must no less lend its assistance, to compose and secure them.

Before concluding this branch of my subject, let me observe, that in manufactures where colours are used, whether by dyeing or by printing, every resource of chemical science is brought into action, to secure brilliancy, permanence, and delicacy of contrast. The whole theory of colour, also, its gradations and subdivisions, are carefully studied, so as to bring this application of colour to frailer textures very near to contact with decorative art.*

* See Neill's "Dictionary of Calico-printing." e. g., p. 64.

Other points of contact will occur to us later; in the meantime, I hasten forward to treat, though hurriedly, of Sculpture.

II.—SCULPTURE.

Sculpture has certain disadvantages compared with Painting. First, in the total absence of colour. For, colour not only gives great beauty, but also lends great assistance, to a work of Art, in producing effects almost to illusion. Another disadvantage is the absence of backgrounds, and of accessories, which also help to carry the eye away from any small defect in the principal objects of the picture. And besides that, it is not capable of combining a large number of figures, brought together in a common action. A group of even three is rare, and is often considered a triumph of Art in Sculpture, as were Gibson's well-known early pieces of classical sculpture. One like the "Dirce," into which several large figures enter, is almost a prodigy.

The artist, therefore, selects a subject sufficiently expressed by one or two figures, and concentrates his entire thought and skill on that small compass, knowing that the eye will be entirely and undistractedly occupied upon them, with no false light—nothing but the pure light of heaven, to give him shadow. Then his work must exhibit, not surface artificially simulating projections or curves, but natural fulness and roundness of the forms he represents; and has to be accurate and correct, not on one side only, but on all; so that all parts shall combine and harmonize one with another, from whatever point they are seen.

But having thus once taken his stand against these disadvantages, the sculptor holds the power of the most noble and glorious performances. He can give form with all completeness of beauty, and expression with all the depth of sentiment; without any danger of the mind's being led astray, or distracted, from that which he expressly intends it to contemplate. His is, in truth, a most noble art. He deals almost exclusively with all that has grandeur or beauty in the supremest of earthly beings. And then, as he works, he feels that what proceeds from his hands, so far as aught human can be, is durable—it is perennial—it is immortal. It hands down the likeness of a great man, or the performance of a great deed, unimpaired, as a monument, or a lesson, to the latest posterity.

Let us now ask, What are its contacts with Science? The first that I will name is one, we may say, almost with pure mathematics. From the time of Michelangelo, though undoubtedly the feeling is much more ancient, there has been an expression of the thought, that the human figure is perfect in its proportions, and that those proportions must have a law. Further study, perfected in our days, has shown this to be truly the case; that the whole of the human figure is ruled by lines, the angles of which are all harmonic—so musical, that they may be represented as tonic, and mediant, and dominant, and in fact by all other proportions of the vibrative string; therefore, that there is in the proportions of the human frame a harmony—a true complete harmony. Besides these harmonic angles, the curves which circumscribe subdivisions possess this quality no less than the angles.

But further still, it is interesting to find, that the curve which dominates through the wonderful structure of man should be that curve which rules the heavens, the ellipse; so that we may say, that the figure which circumscribes the great movements of the celestial sphere also binds, and contains within itself, all the graceful action and the sublime expression of the human frame and countenance. This system has been popularised in a very able and simple exposition by a physician, Dr. Symonds, who brings these principles very clearly into a narrow compass. *

And here a thought suggests itself naturally to a reflecting mind, which permit me to express. The coincidences which have been described exist only in man, and in his upright frame; they will fit no inferior creature, even when casually or momentarily erect. The proportions of the chord, whose vibrations produce harmonies, perfect or imperfect, but musical—the curves which regulate the measured, stately dance of the celestial bodies, meet here without any natural connection; they link themselves together in man, and combine to give the laws of his form. Surely they thus constitute him the in-

* "The Principles of Beauty," by John A. Symonds, M.D. Lond., 1857. Drawn, as to this portion of his work, from Mr. Hay's writings.

tellectual centre of this great system, and show him to us as holding the principal place in a harmonious and uniformly connected plan, formed by a transcendent creative wisdom.

Let me now proceed to say a few words upon what is acknowledged to form a necessary connection between Sculpture (and no less Painting) and Science; a study on which it is not necessary to go into details; and I shall therefore treat it very briefly. I mean *Anatomy*.

It is clear that, for either sculpture or painting, the human figure must be studied and well mastered; so that, without a knowledge of this, no one can ever arrive at the exercise of superior Art. When we look at the highest ancient Grecian sculpture, we are startled by singular contrasts. I will keep the Elgin marbles in my eye in what I am saying, because everybody must be more or less familiar with them. You observe, then, there, a striking contrast. You see heads of magnificent placidity and grandeur of organisation, heads of surpassing intellectuality, yet united to bodies apparently of exaggerated muscularity, and salient framework. There were two types clearly familiar to the Grecian artist; and, we may assume, under his daily observation: so that it is difficult to say whether we can even truly realise them. From whom could come the ideal of those marvellous heads?

' Go into the great museum of Rome or Naples, and mark the grand serenity of Sophocles, or Æschines, or Demosthenes; trace this type through the multitude of philosophers, poets, and orators, whose statues or busts yet remain—until the climax, the culminating point, is reached in the sublime beauty of Plato. Such heads were familiar objects; they belonged to men of thought; they may have thought wrong; their philosophy was, no doubt, erroneous—but they were men that thought and felt deeply upon it, who lived, in fact, for nothing else. The type of their class was impressed upon their countenances; so much so, that if you go through any museum, it will not be difficult at once to recognise the bust of a philosopher or a poet of ancient Greece, among a number representing men of any other caste. Such are the heads which you see prevalent in its highest Art—the intellectual model developed beyond what we ordinarily see, in our days of hard labour and varied active pursuits.

Next we contemplate the athletic body, and conclude that its powerful action exhibits the familiar effects of gymnastic training. I speak under correction; but I hardly think it can be entirely so, in such characters as are represented by the figures alluded to. We are prepared to find this result in the representation of their wrestling matches, their chariot races, or their combats in the amphitheatre. There, of course, you will expect to see a bodily development, which we can never expect to witness. But we cannot imagine that great masters saw nothing more than this outward and shallow appearance, in those terrible exhibitions, which formed no doubt the unenviable school of ancient Art. I believe that what the Grecian sculptor knew how to seize, and alone had the opportunity of seizing, was the result of such deep, such unnatural emotions, as, acting outwards from the nobler organs, impressed themselves in that wonderful way, on their exterior covering.

To illustrate my meaning, let me endeavour to put a scene before you. The ancient Romans, especially the lower orders, including the slaves, were very fond of sketching upon the walls of the ante-rooms (as at Pompeii) such scenes as interested them most; and the greater part of them represent battles of gladiators. These stood in the place of horse-racing, with us; and the people commemorated evidently, and discussed every event of the amphitheatre, as now-a-days they take an interest in what they would have considered, our less-exciting pastime.

These "scratchings" (*graffiti*), as they are called by Father Garrucci, present to us a class of very rude, but very interesting monuments. One of them records a peculiar occurrence. It is indeed only a battle in the amphitheatre, but it is between two men in very different positions; the names of the combatants are given, as they always are, and numbers over their heads tell you how many victories each one had achieved— in other words, how many public murders he had committed. This battle, then, is between Spiculus, a tyro—that is, one who had never before fought, and Aptonetus, *librarius*, or holding a high office among the gladiators—a man who had gained sixteen victories. The first one has over him the letter V—(*vicit*, he conquered); the other, P—(*periit*, he perished). In fact, the old gladiator, with the sixteen laurels that he had won, is lying on the ground wounded to death, or dead; and the youth who has dared to flesh his sword in that old veteran, is alive, and holding his point towards him, perhaps to dispatch him.* Imagine, if you can, the meeting of two such men, without, of course, a particle of moral or noble feeling in their composition; of men who only looked to gaining fame, by the number of murders which they should commit. Imagine the feelings of those two particular men, approaching to meet each other, with the eyes of fifty thousand spectators intent upon them: the one, the old, well-experienced fighter, who is indignant at the idea

* "Les Graffiti de Pompeii," par le Père Garrucci, S. J., Paris, 1856, p. 72, Atlas, plate xiii. This custom of scratching records on the walls, more durable than pencillings, was very general. Most interesting examples have been found in the recent excavations on the Aventine, some of which I gave in a paper published by the R.S.L.; but by far the most valuable are those in the cemetery, or catacomb, of Callistus, discovered by De Rossi. Individual pilgrims of early ages can be traced by them from tomb to tomb; besides, some of more general interest, which have served as clues for discovering lost chambers of that subterranean labyrinth. For example, the resting-place of the martyr-pontiff Sixtus was suggested by these words scratched in the plaster near a blocked-up door: SANCTE SUSTE, ORA PRO ME.

that a stripling like that should have presumed to cope with him, and challenge him to mortal combat ; and the other, feeling that if he can carry off those sixteen laurel crowns upon his sword, he will be sung through all Rome, and celebrated, as those men unfortunately were, by public statues and pictures.* See them approaching one another ; it is a matter of life or death ; one must fall ; one must die. And in that deep silence of the amphitheatre, when even the breath is bated or suppressed by the spectator, they are drawing near with all the caution of a wild beast, that desires not to be seen or heard by the prey, upon which it is going to spring. Yet each of them has boiling in his breast such a storm of passion as we can hardly imagine. What hatred, in that determined resolve to kill as quick as possible his adversary and rival! What a tumult of wicked murderous passion, yet struggled against, by violent repression, to secure coolness, as necessary in that

* A vast hall in the Lateran Palace, now a museum, is paved by a rich mosaic floor, entirely representing full-length portraits of celebrated athletes, with their names, each framed in his separate compartment. What a degradation of Art !

tremendous crisis, filled those breasts, far beyond our power of conception! No shaking of hands before fighting, as with the skilful contenders in the ring; it is a battle to death, in the presence of the whole city.

Can you not conceive how those hearts throbbed and beat, almost audibly; how those lungs dilated themselves convulsively to breathe, to their full expansion; how both these powerful organs, in their vital struggles, would almost force out the bony framework of the chest; how the muscles which were thus quickened would twist themselves into knotted cords, and every vessel that fed them would be gorged with a burning stream, and visibly palpitate to the eyes of the entire audience? And by this violent exertion of the nobler organs, and the concurrent intensity of mental determination, would not a corresponding direction, and almost superhuman vigour, be given to the thews and sinews interested in carrying out the brutal instinct (as in mania, or in sudden catastrophes, where powers unknown or dormant are elicited), so as to impart to even secondary parts, sudden and transient development, swelling and tempering them to steel, for only one tremendous moment.

And then, when the swords clash for an instant, and all those evil passions are more thoroughly concentrated, the blow is scarcely seen; one gleam, as of lightning, flashes, when the swords cross, and one falls a corpse to the ground, or may have to receive still his death-blow from the other. It is impossible to imagine deep-seated, violent emotions under any other circumstances, that could come near to these, or to study their effects upon the human form equally, under any other circumstances.

Yet these were frequently witnessed, and no doubt accurately noted by the keen eye of the sculptor. He had not indeed the opportunity, recollect, that artists have now of studying calmly the muscles of the human body, upon the dissected corpse, or even upon casts taken from it. For Galen himself was obliged thus to study the ape,* in order to come to his approximating knowledge of human anatomy. Thus the processes of learning in ancient and in modern Art are in part reversed. The Greek or Roman arrived at the knowledge of the interior construction of the figure by what he saw without; the modern may learn directly what is concealed by the

* Whewell's "History of the I. S.," vol. iii., p. 392.

outward integuments, and represent its external action. Hence the ancients naturally observed every minute visible change in the human frame; and for contemplating those which our civilization never brings before us—the effects of violent, inhuman passion upon it—they had, unhappily, too many opportunities.*

We may indeed be grateful, and thank heaven, that never again, where the Christian name has penetrated, will there be such a school of Art, or opportunity of arriving at its perfection; if in this it consist, or by these means alone it has to be attained.

Among sciences perfectly modern, the contact of which with both branches of representative Art is greatly desirable, allow me to mention Ethnography. It classifies the different types of races and of nations, and at the same time pays attention to the habits, manners and customs of different countries.

* This topic might be much further illustrated than it could be incidentally in this lecture. Canova's pugilists in Rome, compared with the Grecian works alluded in the text, would show the marked distinction between the development of muscular strength by training, learnt and copied from models, and that might which only strong emotion can produce, as witnessed under their influence.

Begun as a subject of study, having its own interests, and without the least reference to Art, this most important science endeavoured to divide mankind into distinct families, chiefly by the two characteristics of language and of form. Not only the shape of the skull, but the colour of the skin, the texture of the hair, the angles of the eyes, the setting of the limbs, have been taken into calculation in this inquiry. Nay, as I have intimated, the manner of life, in cities, kraals, tents or waggons, the clothing and its decorations, and the artificial disfigurements of the person, receive their due weight in reaching accurate conclusions.

The ancients, from Aristotle downwards, could not be insensible to those characteristic distinctions; nor were they forgotten in Art. In even Egyptian and Assyrian monuments we can distinguish natives from foreigners by their physical varieties, as well as by their attire. The Greeks probably would make the same distinction, whenever they condescended to introduce barbarians into their paintings. And in sculpture, the Phrygian or Persian is distinguished most markedly by his costume, features, &c.*

* Even in the catacombs this distinction is preserved; as,

But in revived Art this was but little attended to. The swarthy and wiry inhabitants of the desert would be represented as fair and plump, and richly draped, as the most civilized and courtly member of the Caucasian family. We behold, in most solemn scenes, as king or magistrate, a turbaned Mussulman merchant caught on the Rialto, or a portly burgomeister who ruled over the destinies of some Dutch village.

This will no longer do. The exacter study of national types, and a more popular acquaintance with them, through greater intercourse, make accurate truthfulness more necessary, in proportion as it is accessible. And it is gratifying to see attention to this point manifestly growing; and not only the human form, and its appurtenances, but the vegetation and peculiarity of rock and soil, made matter of conscientious study, in treating a subject belonging to other climates, and other ages.

As to Sculpture, the Exhibition which has just closed presented two remarkable statues in the Roman court, in which this study has been

for example, in the painting of SS. Abdon and Sennen, Persians, in the cemetery of Pontianus.

carefully attended to. I allude to Mr. Storey's Cleopatra, and African Sibyl; in both of which the artist (an American) has endeavoured to preserve the national type of the Egyptian features, but at the same time to impart the character and expression of more classical models. I believe we may consider that the effort was successful, and embodied a happy thought, realized in sculpture for the first time.

I have spoken of a great science in Ethnography; but surely the artist ought to be ready to descend lower; and to take lessons from Science, of whatever character. It may be vulgar, if you please; but one must get at truth, when scenes have to be represented, as must sometimes be, in which even, by way of contrasts to what is noble and grand, lower and more homely have to be introduced.

We have a worthy example of this artistic condescension in Schiller, who certainly was a word-painter, if ever there was one. Two of his ballads represent such scenes. One of them, the beautiful and touching story of "Fridolin" (*Der Gang nach dem Eisenhammer*), has its scene partly laid, in iron-works with a burning furnace. These he describes in words noted on the spot. We are told that he went to them and studied them; he saw exactly what he describes, and he did not consider it beneath him, to examine minutely the operation which he wished to put in verse.

But there is another, a more noble, and perhaps better known ballad of his, which has gained him immortality—that is, "the Song of the Bell;" imitated by Longfellow, in his "Building of the Ship." It may present itself to our imagination as a double chain, interchangeably winding round each other—the one of gold, and the other of silver; so that first one of the strands, and then the other, comes before the eye. For in it he describes very exactly the process by which the bell is cast, from beginning to end. But with this he blends, in alternate stanzas, the uses to which the bell will be put, in peace and in war, in religion and in crime, in gladness and in sorrow, in public and in domestic life. There could not be a more exquisite piece of work than this; and not the smallest portion of its beauty consists in the extreme accuracy with which the more technical part of it is managed. He has made it so perfect, that you might almost cast a bell from his account; yet there are certainly few poems which give a groundwork for more beautiful pictures.*

A great poet, then, was not above studying common subjects, or the mechanical operations of practical Science, when he had to introduce them into his verses. Why should not an artist be of the same mind, despising nothing which can give reality or truth to what he represents?

I fear I may not have interested you as much as I wish; so I will venture to illustrate what I have suggested, on the humble condescending of Art, to learn from meaner pursuits, by two anecdotes, one relating to Sculpture, and the other to Painting. And if they descend rather from the dignity of my subject, you will at least allow that they are very practical exemplifications of it.

A friend of mine, many years ago, told me —in fact I was in Rome at the time—that he had brought with him an English servant, who knew nothing upon earth of Art in any branch, and, though very honest and faithful, was perfectly stolid on that subject. In fact, there was only one topic on which he was considered

---

* A large and beautiful engraving, illustrative of the song, has been made by Schleich from designs by Nielson.

to be what is called "knowing," that was, one instinctive to men of his county (for he was from Yorkshire), *hippology*, or the science of horses. His master took him through the Vatican Museum; as he went along, he looked at things with the most unmeaning eyes, until they came to the Sala della Biga, in the centre of which beautiful rotunda is a most perfect model in marble of an ancient chariot, drawn by two horses, running evidently at full speed, with distended nostrils and dishevelled manes, whether in battle or in the race. "Now," said my friend to his attendant, "look at these two horses, and tell me what you think of them." He was delighted, he brightened up immediately, and just as if his master had told him to buy a pair of horses at some fair in Holderness or Craven, he set about his commission most scientifically. He patted kindly their marble necks and flanks, stroked gently their stony coats, and examined them round and round at all points. "Now," asked his master, "what do you say to those horses?" "Why, sir, *that* is a splendid animal; I don't think much of t'other." Now, he had just hit the right thing; the first was the antique, the ancient horse, and the other the modern restoration. There was truly a scientific test applied, and probably no connoisseur, or even artist, would have come so well out of the difficulty.

My other illustration applies to Painting. In the late Manchester Exhibition there was a very large picture, which I believe was a fresco by Lattanzio Gambara, of Brescia (1541-74), cut out of a wall, representing the death of Absalom. On one side, the young Jewish prince was represented as hanging by his hair from the branches of an oak; and, on the other, the mule which he had been riding, was galloping away, looking scared and wild. An acquaintance of mine was looking at this picture, when two men came up, who evidently belonged to the same profession as our former critic, no doubt equally versed in all equine topics. They gazed upon it for some time in silence, when one of them broke out with an exclamation which startled my friend to attention. "Well, he thoroughly deserves it!" "Why so?" "Why, what a stupid fellow he must have been, to think of riding such a vicious brute as that—with nothing but a snaffle!"

You see that neither the sculptor nor the

painter, in these instances, should have been above getting the opinion of some one who, although no artist, could give him scientific information on any matter wherein he was practically versed. May we not say, that no equestrian statue should ever be executed, and set up as a public monument, without its model having been as carefully examined, by a professional judge, as is a valuable horse before it is purchased? The public exhibition by Apelles of a great picture, on which every one was at liberty to make his remarks, and to point out, first defects, and then excellencies, was, to judge from the proverb to which it gave rise,* intended

---

* "*Sutor ne supra crepidam!*" "Let not the shoemaker go *higher* than the sandal." As Pliny tells the story, a shoemaker, examining the picture, remarked, that there was a loop too few in the inside of the Greek sandal (*crepida*), which was fastened by thongs. Next day, proud of having discovered a real defect, he ventured to criticise something in the leg; when Apelles indignantly leapt from behind the panel, where he had been secretly listening to all faultfinders, and addressed the presumptuous craftsman in the words quoted, which became proverbial in Greek and Latin. (H. N. L., xxx., 10.) We have totally destroyed the point and history of the proverb, by substituting *last* for *sandal*. As to equestrian statues, there was a celebrated dispute, I believe, whether an eminent sculptor had not represented wrong, the order of motion in the horse's feet.

to ellicit such professional remarks upon accessories, on which a painter could not well be suppposed to be fully instructed. This denoted the sincere desire of a truly great artist to be minuitely accurate.

Our conclusion, in fact, must be, that a great artistt not only should despise no branch of knowledge, but should endeavour to acquire every variety of it. If I remember right, Mr. Ruskin has observed, that a painter should be a man of universal learning. This is what Cicero has said of the finished orator; and can hardly be less true of the artist. The higher and more varied the education he can receive, the more extensive the learning which he acquires, the more it will assist him in his artistic pursuits, to attain truth in copying nature, and reality in depicting life. " *Ut pictura poësis*—as painting so is poetry," says the Roman critic, who adds,

"Ego nec studium sine divite vena,
Nec rude quid possit video ingenium ; alterius sic
Altera poscit opem res, et conjurat amice." *

---

* " I see not what, without true genius, study,
Nor genius without study, can effect.
Each needs each; both, when hand in hand, will thrive."
HORACE, A. P. 409.

III.—ARCHITECTURE.

In proceeding to address you, as concisely as possible, on Architecture, it may seem superfluous to observe, that it obviously divides itself into two branches—the purely artistic, and the constructive or scientific.

If on the one side it seems to descend towards the class of mechanical pursuits, on the other it rises so high as to command its other two sisters, and to be almost necessary for their perfect existence. I have sufficiently intimated, that one great difference between ancient and modern Art, including Mediæval Art under the first division, consists in this—that ancient Art was public, and modern is private. Galleries of Sculpture were anciently unknown; its most matchless pieces were in temples or in public halls, such as those of baths, or in open gardens perhaps adorning fountains; but generally accessible to the most plebeian eye. For this end great public buildings were necessary, and in former ages were ever amply provided. But this very circumstance shows how Architecture is in the highest sense a Fine Art, and must always necessarily grow, as such, commensurately with the advancement of the other two branches of the Arts of Design.

The treasures of Sculpture which England possesses are undoubtedly the Elgin Marbles. Yet what were they but subordinate to the building which they adorned? The sculptor limited and compressed his superb metopes to fit into architectural spaces designed and commanded by the architect, and lengthened his frieze (by, to him perhaps, tedious repetition) to the measures and proportions prescribed to him. But, more wonderfully still, the sublime artist shaped, and bent, and cut off portions of his splendid figures, though finished as carefully on the shoulders as on the chest, and even where the projecting cornice must have hidden their beauties, so as to fit and adapt them to the slopes of the tympanum; till they diminished to the emerging heads of Aurora's steeds—heads that make us fancy he must have almost felt indignant at not being allowed room for equally matchless bodies. But how could such an artist have lent himself to the adornment, or rather the work, of such a building, unless he had felt it to be worthy of him? How could his genius have bowed and adapted itself to any but a kindred, and avowedly equal, one? It was necessary indeed that Architecture, in its artistic character, as capable of satisfying and gratifying the eye, should have been on a level with Sculpture, to have so secured its confidence, co-operation, and almost subordination, through the very masterpieces of its skill.

And the same must be said of Painting. With few, and not perfectly successful, exceptions, we are content with easel paintings to hang upon the walls of private houses or even of galleries. The latter, indeed, as public buildings, ought to give ample scope to Architecture, and at Florence or Munich they have done so. But in most countries chance buildings have been adapted or adopted, to give a home to Pictorial Art.* Yet, as I have

* In Rome there is no gallery of paintings, properly so called; the two public collections date from a recent period. The writer remembers the small but invaluable one in the Vatican, in four different parts of the palace. The hall which the principal pictures occupied before the last change to a warmer and brighter position, from having sun, is being covered by Podesti with immense frescoes. But the great rooms and corridors, painted by Raffaele and his scholars, are open to the public, peasant as well as noble. And these are where they were painted; a nobler gallery could not well be built or becomingly furnished.

already observed, Painting on a great scale, and for public instruction, requires great wall-spaces, expressly provided for it by the architect.

And now, considering Architecture, in its first aspect, as a Fine Art, I may repeat what I have said of the human figure; for the proportions and parts of its perfect productions are no less tonic or musical; lines and angles —there being here no curves—are reducible to the same harmonic scale.

The Parthenon, that grandest of classical edifices, which was considered by the greatest of sculptors worthy of being adorned by his chisel, has been most accurately measured in all its parts by an English architect, sent expressly for this purpose. It is upon his measurements that the reduction has been made; and it has been found that all the lines and angles in it are harmonic or tonic, without a jar or dissonance among them, so that musical chords could be constructed from its proportions. The same treatment has been applied to Lincoln, and later to Salisbury, cathedral; and it has been ascertained no less that all the angles (being much more angular buildings, of course, than the Grecian one) have the same properties, and are

F

reducible to similar principles. These coincidences show that, though no doubt the men who designed and built those great edifices had no idea of the science which they obeyed, they had it in their eye—they had it in their feeling; so that when Science came in, and tested their work, she verified and found it strictly according to its rules.*

Nowhere, however, does Science come so directly into contact with Art as in the constructive element of Architecture. And this in two ways:—

The first is in the selection and even the preparation of materials. Where experience has not fully guaranteed the material proposed for a building, or a new one is to be preferred, the decision of its value or fitness clearly belongs to Science.

This was acknowledged, and acted upon, when this nation resolved to erect an edifice which might be considered as its Capitol—a monument not national, but European, to its constitutional principles and life. No expense

---

* See Dr. Symonds's work quoted above, p. 23; from Mr. Hay's "Orthographic Beauty of the Parthenon," 1853.

was to be spared; competition led to the selection of a consummate architect, with a splendid design: its exterior was to be encrusted with sculpture; its interior enriched with paintings; so as to make it more than a museum—not a collection of past, but a record of present, Art.

The first step, in proceeding to execute this magnificent idea, was to secure its solidity and permanency. Most wisely, therefore, a commission was formed, comprising, besides architects, eminent men of Science, geologists and chemists, who were to select the best stone for the building. The Dolomite, or Magnesian Limestone, which had proved so durable in the Jermyn Street Museum, was selected to be taken from the Bolsover Quarries, in Nottinghamshire. But the recommendation made by the scientific men was not carried out;* another

* In one important respect, however, the scientific recommendation was based upon error. It was supposed by Sir H. de la Beche, that York, Beverley, and Ripon Minsters were built of Dolomite; whereas they were constructed of "Yorkshire stone." (Sir R. I. Murchison, in "Report of Commission, 1861," 471.) A further mistake was, that Southwell Church, the Norman carvings of which are intact, was built with Bolsover stone. This fact, however, on which

stone was selected. The following answer, in an examination before a later committee, is like a key to the whole result:—"We (the builders) did not look at the stone with the eyes of chemists, we looked at it as builders."* Stone more convenient for building with, as being better stratified, but from the same range of rock, was preferred; and what has been the result?

A new commission had to be issued in 1861, to examine into the causes of the rapid decay, which has attacked and gnawed the stone-work of that splendid building, on every side. Negative results have been easily obtained. Not elevation, nor exposure, not proximity to the fetid river, not aspect towards the pottery-smoke of the opposite bank—no distinguishable circumstance which can give a clue to particular chemical or mechanical action, in atmosphere or weather, has been yet determined on, as an adequate cause of this natural dilapidation.

Melancholy, indeed, is the Report issued of the actual condition of things. It is too long

much stress is laid, is subject, at least, to grave doubts. (See Appendix to Report, p. 100.)

* Ib., p. 19. See Report. p. 7.

to quote. Suffice it to say, that signs of decay manifested themselves in seven years after the building commenced, and even much earlier opposite Henry VIIth's chapel; that it cannot be accounted for by exposure to the weather, being worst in sheltered situations; and that the mischief yet in store, and not apparent, is very considerable.* Chemical expedients have been recommended, and are being tried; to give an artificial hardness to the decaying stones, and arrest, by surface-washes, the disintegration of solid rock.

Is it too much to say, that this example proves the desirableness of more decided and friendly contact, between Science and Art? Is it not to be feared, that they have not fully understood one another? Does it not appear that the terms of mutual correspondence were not clear and definite; that there was no subordination of one to the other, or of harmonious co-operation between them?

The necessity for this good understanding will, no doubt, be gradually better attended to. For nothing can be more wise, sensible, and straightforward, than the conclusion come to

* P. v.

by the Committee, with which I will close this topic.

"They" (the chemists) "recommend that a series of chemical experiments should be conducted, *under chemical supervision* for a considerable period of time; and the Committee are most reluctantly compelled to coincide with them."*

I have alluded to the possible case of new and untried materials for building being required. In our days, this is no hypothesis. Iron has become a material, without which it is doubtful whether any future architect will be able to execute a great work. As a substitute for timber, and for the older vaulting, its place is definite and indisputable. Can it become a manageable material for decorative art, and so an architectural resource? Why not? It is, no doubt, inferior in estimation, and in the value-order of metals, to bronze or copper. Yet it is gradually usurping one of the hitherto exclusive offices of those richer substances, by emulating their sonorousness. Steel is beginning to rival and supplant the costlier material in the bell. Iron is more abundant, more gene-

* P. viii.

rally understood, and, above all, more accessible and economical.*

Its affinity for oxygen, and consequent facility of corrosion, is yet its greatest defect. But if we intend to have artistic buildings multiplied, and consequently require a manageable material, to be employed on a wide scale; if casting in metal will be found an easier process for multiplication of good models than carving in stone: then Chemistry will come to assist Art in preparing the new material desired.

The beautiful specimens which Berlin has exhibited of iron manufacture, possessing all the delicacy of precious metal work, show the perfect fusibility of the coarser material, whether obtained by the addition of phosphorus and arsenic, or by a more careful purification. And after chemistry has thus enabled iron to attain the sharpness of bronze, she will easily veil it with a coating of some metal exempt from the same avidity for oxygen, not to disguise poverty, but for the legitimate end of preservation.

* The drinking-fountains of the metropolis have given examples, not very favourable ones, of artistic applications of iron.

The second point in constructive Architecture, where it is not merely in contact with Science, but becomes a part of it, is in the adjustment of ·weight and support—the balancing of the parts of the building.

Looking anywhere at the first stages of Architecture, we are astonished at the massiveness of their construction, at the immense thickness of their walls and pillars. We find this character in the old Grecian; we find it in the Roman; we find it in the Etruscan; and later we find it in the Norman, or Roman, style, as it is called in some parts of Europe. We have huge supports sustaining indeed great masses, but far beyond the exigencies of the case. We admire this ponderous solidity very much now; but in reality it is probably the result of timidity or ignorance. The early builders could not calculate the proportion requisite between superincumbent weight and its just support; and they erred on the right side, by providing superabundant strength, to carry their intended burthen. We observe how, by degrees, every architecture becomes slimmer and lighter, as experience has brought these proportions to test; hence, after the Doric comes the Ionic, then we get to the Corinthian, and, at last, to the Composite. In like manner we pass from the Norman, through intermediate stages of pointed architecture, to the Flamboyant or Decorated.

Remarkable evidence remains, how the heavier construction of remoter periods was not based upon any accurate calculation of ratio between support and weight; but that the first went much beyond the demands of the second. In several churches we surprise, in a manner, the architects of the sixteenth century, in the act of altering the old-fashioned Norman arch into the pointed, and the round massive piers into slender clustered columns; thus cutting out masses of sustaining material, without apprehension of insecurity. This is the case at Ripon, where the chancel-arch has been entirely transformed on one side; and at St. Alban's, where a few years more of ecclesiastical peace would have seen the entire church so changed.

At the period of decay in Roman architecture, as in the churches built by Galla Placidia, at Ravenna, we find the expedient adopted, of constructing the vaults with terra-cotta hollow cylinders, which, simulating solid masonry, gave extreme lightness to the supported structure, yet have proved durable enough to stand till now intact.

I do not know that I can better illustrate this portion of my subject, or give a more striking instance of intervention most salutary, because uncontrolled, of Science, in a matter which belongs so essentially to Architecture, than that which occurs in the history of St. Peter's in Rome. You are aware, of course, and I need not therefore describe it, what a matchless edifice is the dome of St. Peter's. Its shape every one can understand who has seen that of St. Paul's, in London; though the proportions are a great deal more grand. It was the crowning work of Michelangelo, though afterwards there was superadded a lantern, which did not enter into his plan, but added materially to the original weight.

There is a popular idea current, that Michelangelo made the huge piers, on which the dome had to rest, so exactly proportioned to the weight they had to bear, that he even made a dying request, that they should never be touched; that they were afterwards perforated to make some staircases and niches, and that the consequence was, that the whole dome was threatened with ruin. All this is incorrect, as I will show you just now. It is not likely that Michelangelo, whose characteristic was massiveness to excess, would have so offended. But in addition, it deserves to be mentioned, that at the time when he built these piers, a commission was appointed, of which I believe Raffaele was a member, to examine them; and that their report was, that the piers should be still further strengthened. Immensely deep wells were accordingly sunk at their feet, and filled with Roman concrete—which is the strongest, I suppose, in the world—so as to give great additional support.

It will be useful, to give you the exact dimensions, in English feet, of the great masses concerned in what I am about to speak of:

Piers, on which the dome rests, 282 round.
Cupola, diameter, 141½.
Circumference, about 423.
Height of *arches*, on which it rests, from the pavement, 146.*
Height of lower edge of *dome*, 171½.
Total height to *summit of lantern*, 446½.†

---

* The real foundation is, of course, lower, as the piers pass through the crypt or *sotterraneo*, under the church.

† "Rome, a Tour of Many Days," by Sir G. Head, vol. iii., pp. 223, 255.

Perhaps the greatest promise ever made by Art, and faithfully kept, was here. Michelangelo is said to have declared that he would raise the Pantheon up into the skies. These dimensions show how he kept his word.

About 1681, it was observed that there were numerous cracks in various directions, through the cupola; and great blame was thrown upon Bernini, who was accused of having made dangerous staircases and niches in the piers; however, his friend and biographer, Baldinucci, produced plans of earlier date, in which these alterations were marked; thus disproving that Bernini had been their author. He moreover speaks of the fissures then apparent as trifling. But they went on increasing. What are called in Italy seals—that is, marble dove-tails, were placed across the cracks; and these broke, or were breaking with alarming rapidity. It was evident that the work of destruction was going on; and before the middle of the last century, it was feared that, in a few years more, the whole dome of St. Peter's might fall in.

Architects came forward, to suggest various

remedies for the threatened evil. One wanted to block up the windows, another to make great spurs or buttresses, in addition to the columns that surround the cupola, to give it strength. In truth, the whole structure would have been disfigured, by the proposed expedients; but in reality, it was difficult to find a remedy. Benedict XIV., a most able and learned man, was Pope at the time. He wisely observed, that this was not the business of Art, but that belonged to Science. So he named a special commission of three mathematicians—pure mathematicians, having nothing to do with building or architecture, to examine the case. When I mention their names, scientific persons will easily understand how they were selected.

At the head of the commission was Father Boscovich, a Jesuit, who had twice measured arcs of the meridian, and had published a number of works on Astronomy, on the spots on the Sun, on Optics, and many other philosophical subjects; a man, in truth, of European reputation, and one of the first men in Italy who accepted the Newtonian system. The other two were not Jesuits, but religious of another order.

They were the editors of what is commonly called the Jesuits' Edition of Newton, Le Sueur, and Jacquier; men purely and exclusively scientific. How did they go about their work? As scientific men would naturally do, with great care and caution, as well as ability.

As they drew up a minute report of their proceedings, under the modest title of "Opinion of Three Mathematicians,"* and presented it to the Pope, I have only to abridge their own account of them. It was given in at the close of 1742; and they commence their paper by apologising for apparently intruding into a province not their own, and pleading for their excuse the sovereign command; showing, at the same time, how Science has properly to deal with such a matter.

Their first care was to examine most minutely the entire dome, within and without, and form thus a plan of all the injuries which it had suffered. They give an accurate list of thirty-two distinct damages, some very severe, and running

---

* "Parere di tre mattematici, sopra i danni che si sono trovati nella cupola di San Pietro, sul fine dell' anno 1742." It contains diagrams, and sections, which illustrate every part of the text.

in various directions. The stone lintels over several of the windows were split in two. And when they applied a plumb-line to the buttress-pillars round the drum, or cylinder, of the dome, these proved to be as much as over an inch, out of the perpendicular.

This naturally pointed to the over-pressure of the spheroidal portion, with the lantern above, upon the drum. But our three Mathematicians were not satisfied with this simple deduction; they carefully examined the piers to which popular judgment attributed the damage; and they found that judgment to be erroneous. The piers were intact, and required no attention. They therefore advised that nothing should be done to them. Thus having formed the hypothesis of over-pressure, they proved that every phenomenon, to the slightest crack, fell into it, and was adequately explained by it, and by no other.

Their next step was to verify most exactly the reality of what they had theoretically ascertained, by weighing, on the one hand, the materials supported, and measuring, on the other, the sustaining power. I will not detain you with details, which are minutely given in the original Memoir, but present to you the general results. Having exactly weighed measured portions of the materials, used in the construction of this wonderful building—the stone, brick, copper, lead, and iron—and then, from accurate plans, and by sound calculations, having measured the quantity of each, they found that the entire dome, with its lantern, came to the frightful weight of 165 millions of Roman pounds, or 55,245 tons.

They obtain separately the weight of the gravitating portion; and then calculate the resistance or supporting powers. This consisted, first, in the drum (*tamburro*), with its pillars thrust already out of the perpendicular; and secondly, of an iron girder, too slight for its purpose, but so embedded in the wall, that it could not be examined. They estimate, however, its tenacity, and take it into reckoning; but conjecture that it had either snapped or dilated, so as to be useless.

But they thus reached the awful result—that there was a balance of five million pounds, or 1,674 tons, on the side of pressure against support. The conclusion of the Mathematicians was, "that an irreparable ruin was reasonably to be apprehended, unless a timely and efficient remedy were applied." *

We may well imagine the alarm of Rome, with its artistic population, at such an announcement as this; and at hearing that this collapse and ruin had only been prevented so far, by an iron collar round the base of the lantern, and by the peculiar construction which united the double dome to this, so as to prevent its falling out.

It is easier to find a defect, and prognosticate misfortune, than to remedy the one, or to avert the other. But the commission to the three Mathematicians was, not only to probe the evil, but also to suggest its " efficient cure," which they consequently proceeded to do.

Well, what sort of a remedy did they suggest? One entirely scientific, and not a little appalling. It was to put six more solid girders round this huge periphery of 420 feet. Each, of course, was to be divided into several sections, or arcs; and where these met, each had to branch into three; and these branches proceeding from the two arcs, were to be fastened by bolts passing through sockets in them; the bolts again being riveted

* P. xxx.

to chains passed round the building. A gigantic or Cyclopean undertaking; for you must remember that there were then and there no Nasmyth's hammers, or Birmingham rolling-mills; so that the enormous hoops had all to be forged and shaped by hand.

Of course, no sooner had this Report appeared than it was assailed in all its parts—groundwork, deductions, and proposals.* To vindicate it, and reply to the objections so gravely urged, and, at the same time, give an account of further proceedings in the matter, a second Memoir was drawn up by the same learned men, early in the following year. A meeting of the general committee was then held, comprising architects, antiquarians, and others. A fresh examination was made; and finally the decision of the "three mathematicians" was adopted, and their proposal accepted.†

* Among other assailants was Lelio Cosatti. "Rifflessioni sopra il parere dei tre mattematici," Rome, 1743. He attributes the damages to a general and gradual giving way or settlement, throughout the building, and to the action of lightning and earthquakes. He deprecates all interference with the dome.

† The general committee to which the scientific Report was referred, closely interrogated its authors on every point, and had scaffolding erected in the dome to enable its mem-

There was no time to be lost, and no time *was* lost. Before the end of that year, 1743, two girders were braced round the drum. In 1744, three more were added. According to Poleni, their weight amounted to 119,044 Roman pounds, or 39 tons.*

In 1747 it was found that the "mathematicians" had conjectured rightly, that the girder put in under Sixtus V. had sprung; and another was substituted for it. These iron circles are not visible, but are imbedded in the stone-work.

We have here a notable instance of Science coming to the succour, or rather to the rescue, of Art, in one, certainly, of its most painful crises. One knows not which most to admire; the sagacity which at once recognised the power that was needed and called it in, or the free and unlimited scope given to its exercise, or the sensible acquiescence of the artistic commissioners, or the

bers to visit the damages with safety. One or two dissentients only delayed their votes till they could examine everything personally. The principal one, I believe, was Arringhi, the great explorer of the Catacombs.

* "Beschreibung der Stadt Rom." Zw. B., p. 208. I may mention, that the objection advanced, that thirty-nine tons more weight was proposed to be added to the already enormous mass of the dome, is fully met in the second Memoir.

sound judgment of the scientific deputation, or, finally, the complete success of its remedy.

Without this all else, and a vast expense, would have been wasted. But the proposed cure fully answered; and now, after 120 years, no sign has been given of subsequent damage; but the seals, or dovetails, placed over the former fissures, left purposely open, are unbroken and unmoved.

I must now hasten in earnest to my conclusion. Having spoken so much of the assistance afforded by Science to Art, is it to be understood that, on the other hand, Art is to do nothing for Science? Certainly not. Wishing to be very brief, I can do no more than allude to a new branch of Art, though intimately connected with Science; and remind you of what Photography has lately done for Astronomy? I am sure that every one here knows Mr. Warren de la Rue's accurate and beautiful Photographs, which have thrown so much real light upon the phenomena of the last great eclipse. Art is taking portraits of the sun and of the moon, and other celestial bodies. It is thus coming forward materially to second Science; and no doubt there will be many other ways in which the assistance will be found to be mutual. Points of contact are often only points of repulsion: may they be here points of attraction and cohesion.

Let me, therefore, unhesitatingly remark, that these two, Art and Science, must advance united, and yet be each independent. This was one of the thoughts well and often put forth by the lamented Prince Consort. We may say, that the two have to carry forward the arts of life, and the arts of production, those arts which govern, which, in things material, enrich and refine, society. They are like two feet, such as the creative Wisdom has given to every human creature, to the only one of sentient beings on earth who can stand erect, and raise his countenance to heaven. If the two feet attempt to move at once, or if they are bound together, a fall of both, with the whole body, may be safely predicted. If one pretends to move on alone, it will find it has no power of progress; it will advance, but the body will always remain with the one that lags behind. It is necessary that this should not only reach, but pass beyond its friendly and concordant rival, or rather its companion, for real forward advance to be obtained. And thus Art and

Science should go together, belonging to the same body, animated by the same spirit, obeying in reality the same principle of life and action; but at the same time each proceeding in its own motion, according to its own laws, waiting the other patiently, or, if necessary, going beyond it, to make it follow; so that this happy competition tend to the concurrent advance of both.

They must be as two eyes: they must look at the same object; their nerves must decussate, in order that they may unite in impressions and sensations; while the muscles, which move each, remain separate and distinct. There must be consent, but not identity, of action between them.

They have different modes of progression. Art is quick, is rapid; it has the power of making wings pullulate in a moment, from itself, and giving them at once growth and impulse, to fly out of the grasp of Science. Science must be content to walk on its feet, feeling every inch of ground on which it treads, before it can presume to go a step further. And if I were to say that the one has the velocity of the hare, spoken of in the well-known apologue, let not the other disdain being compared to the tortoise; which, in old cosmogonies, is represented as bearing the whole weight of the cosmic system. The course of Science is indeed slower; but it will always, when wanted, overtake Art.

I will venture to illustrate this point from two sources, but very concisely. Divine Providence has granted to this country the immense privilege of having made two of the greatest discoveries that the world has ever known; the one, that by which Newton enthroned, in the midst of our system, the sun as its lord and regulator; the other that of Harvey, who enshrined the heart in the middle of the little world (the *microcosm*) which each of us possesses. Both have led to consequences which strike us with amazement, and can, indeed, hardly be too highly prized.

If any one will pursue the history of light, as at present established, in the theory of undulations, and see what minute steps have been necessary, to reach certainty on this point, in the course of nearly two hundred years; how the smallest discovery, polarization, depolarization, periodical colour, fringed shadows, striated surfaces, double refraction, thick or thin plates, even to the child's soap-bubble—has been of value as a stepping-stone in induction, until at last the present doctrine has been established; he will be almost awe-struck, though charmed, by the patience, the perseverance, and the healthy tone and power of Science, no less than by its well-earned triumphs.

If next we turn to the newer field which is just opening, and see what is being done with light; how the recent observations on the solar spectrum have brought together two sciences, which by their natures seemed most remote one from the other—Optics, which requires that its objects should be distant; and Chemistry, which demands that they should be in contact, and have created, of the two, one, by the pursuit of which we are approaching and gaining discoveries of immense beauty and value: when we consider how, in 1802, Fraunhoffer discovered lines that went across the prismatic spectrum, and marked their unvarying places, and that it has been only nearly sixty years afterwards that those little lines, multiplied into thousands by Sir D. Brewster, have become the key to the most elegant and astonishing discoveries of modern times about the sun, we shall acknowledge how untiring, how unrepining, but how certain, has Science been in its onward progress.

The very substance and atmosphere of the sun have been brought into the laboratory, have been put into the crucible, analysed, and humbled to the level of terrestrial substances, by the chemists of Heidelberg.* Only, the great painter is no more who would have almost ventured to depict his face with earthly colours.

The other grand discovery to which I have alluded, that of Harvey, has been as fertile, almost, in beautiful, as in profitable results. From the moment that the double circulation in the body was established as a truth, equal in its completeness to that of the sun's place in the firmament, what an application of Science has followed in its train; how have chemistry, mechanics, hydrostatics, found their principles, and most wonderful illustrations, in the functions of life. How have infinitely varied forms of transmutation, and new combination, been analysed,

* A simple and intelligible, yet very complete, account of all the discoveries on the solar spectrum, to the close of last year, has been published by M. Radau, in the "Annuaire du Cosmos" for this year.

and their organs exactly defined; how has the structure of every substance, every texture and tissue, been submitted to the penetrating scrutiny of the microscope; till every portion, however small, of the human frame is discovered to be instinct with living energy, which carries on mysterious operations, necessary for existence; without consciousness, in him who furnishes all the ingredients and the instruments, required for their performance. In truth, one inch of the pliant and yielding skin contains more work in its compass than a laboratory; there is a ramification of vessels and nerves, which can hardly escape a needle's point; there are spiral ducts proceeding from minutely fabricated vessels, to convey to the surface the exudation which should lubricate it, and dissipate superfluous humour; subtile ducts, which, on the other hand, absorb into the system what is outside it; an unceasing elaboration, in gradual and rising layers, of the pigment which gives the olive, or copper, or black colour to the skin; and finally, the manufacture of the apparently valueless hair, each filament of which, inimitably spun, springs up like a distillation from its own alembic, having its own capillary feed-pipe from the perennial cistern of the heart, and its own tiny spark of fire from the purifying furnace of the lungs, or rather from the "Vestal flame" of life. And all these exquisite and accurate processes are going on in contact, everywhere, without mutual disturbance or interference.

All this minute investigation, and a thousand others, we may trace, step by step, to the great discovery of our English physician. And these clearer perceptions of the wonders which we need not go beyond each of ourselves to seek, render physiology a study charming and delightful, far beyond any tale of fiction; with which is blended a deep and awful mystery, the mystery of life—the spring of all that beautiful activity, which is only subservient, in man, to higher intellectual processes.

And as to the vaster, though not nobler, parts or domains, of Science, which contemplate the entire universe, not their single contemplator, the pleasure derived from the perusal of their annals—the history of their gradual unfolding, written, as it has been,* in becomingly terse, simple, and magisterial language, is not unlike

* The "History of the Inductive Sciences."

that enjoyed at the unrolling of a richly illuminated vellum, or the reading of a gradually unfolding royal " Idyll."

After these remarks, it is superfluous to ask: Is all this Science, are all these discoveries, to be considered as merely material additions to knowledge, and not also food of the most dainty character, for the highest and purest feelings of man's intellect and heart? Assuredly not. I hope that some one or other will, some day, stand here, much better able to handle such subjects than I am, and give you a lecture on "the Poetry of Science;" and show you how, following its progress, on almost any subject, there is involved in it an epic, often of sublime magnificence: how, especially if we ascend to the heavens, and contemplate what astronomy has now laid open to us; we arrive there at more beautiful realities than even Dante could imagine, when, in his noble poetry, he flitted from star to star, and made each the seat of a peculiar felicity, or of a singular intellectual gift; or than Milton could dream, when in his silence he dwelt upon his lofty conceptions of heavenly beauty, after the outer world had been shut out from his sight, lest it should come like a cross-light athwart the inward ray which brightened up his mental pictures.

Yes; far beyond imagination has been here reality; and such a reality as not only amply repays application, if truth be loved, but such as rewards study where supreme beauty is admired. Science thus not only comes into contact with Art, but blends with it, and combines inseparably; the two are as one, when they follow out their highest joint aim; that of rising to the most perfect, humanly attainable, perception of the uncreated beautiful and the divinely true. To this happy union we may apply the lines of the last-mentioned of our poets:

> " How charming is divine philosophy!
> Not harsh and crabbed, as dull fools suppose,
> But musical as is Apollo's lyre."

THE END.

NEW AND CHEAPER EDITION.

In one volume, crown 8vo, embellished with Portraits, 5s., bound.

RECOLLECTIONS OF
THE LAST FOUR POPES.

BY HIS EMINENCE CARDINAL WISEMAN.

Opinions of the Press.

"A picturesque book on Rome and its Ecclesiastical Sovereigns by an eloquent Roman Catholic. Cardinal Wiseman has here treated a special subject with so much generality and geniality that his Recollections will excite no ill-feeling in those who are most conscientiously opposed to every idea of human infallibility represented by Papal domination."—*Athenæum.*

"These delightful pages are a record of the favourite impressions received by the author from scenes, persons, and events, interesting to all, but pre-eminently so to Catholics."—*Tablet.*

"Among the glories of Rome, these Recollections are not the least." —*Dublin Review.*

"Messrs. Hurst and Blackett have done good service by publishing a newly revised and cheaper edition of His Eminence Cardinal Wiseman's 'Recollections of the last Four Popes.' Such a proceeding sufficiently attests the popularity of this production of the illustrious writer. This historical work is of peculiar interest to English speaking Catholics, as containing much important information which could proceed from no other pen. It is now within the reach of nearly all classes, and although cheap in the ordinary meaning of the term, it is got up in a style that reflects the highest credit upon the publishers. The portraits are especially good, and this new edition may be considered particularly suitable for a Gift Book."— *Weekly Register.*

"This is a new and revised edition of a work upon which criticism has already pronounced its judgment. The accomplished author never fails to invest with interest any subject on which he writes or speaks. It is no wonder, then, that this book should have commanded the attention and, in many respects elicited the approval, of even those who most widely differ with him in his views of the Pontificate, and of the administrative institutions of modern Rome. The new edition of the 'Recollections' is published at, even for this age of cheap literature, the remarkably moderate price of 5s.; though it is a good-sized volume, beautifully printed, and illustrated."—*Sun.*

"Biography is one of the most interesting departments of literature, but it is peculiarly so when derived from personal knowledge, and based on observation. The present work, on account both of its subject and its author, is a literary curiosity, and certainly the expectations which may be formed of it will not be disappointed. Cardinal Wiseman is one of the most eminent dignitaries of the Roman Church, and as such is sure to command a wide audience; but he is also one of the first scholars and ablest writers of the day. In the present work he has kept aloof from controversy; and it must be admitted that on the whole he writes in a free and tolerant spirit. His sketches of Vatican life might have been penned by Benvenuto Cellini, they are so candid and at the same time so graphic. He has done wisely to write his work for all creeds, and it may be read by all with equal profit and interest." —*United Service Magazine.*

HURST AND BLACKETT, PUBLISHERS, 13, GREAT MARLBOROUGH STREET.

Under the Especial Patronage of Her Majesty.

Published annually, in One Vol., royal 8vo, with the Arms beautifully engraved, handsomely bound, with gilt edges, price 31s. 6d.

LODGE'S PEERAGE

AND BARONETAGE,

CORRECTED BY THE NOBILITY.

THE 32nd EDITION FOR 1863 IS NOW READY.

LODGE'S PEERAGE AND BARONETAGE is acknowledged to be the most complete, as well as the most elegant, work of the kind. As an established and authentic authority on all questions respecting the family histories, honours, and connections of the titled aristocracy, no work has ever stood so high. It is published under the especial patronage of Her Majesty, and is annually corrected throughout, from the personal communications of the Nobility. It is the only work of its class in which, *the type being kept constantly standing*, every correction is made in its proper place to the date of publication, an advantage which gives it supremacy over all its competitors. Independently of its full and authentic information respecting the existing Peers and Baronets of the realm, the most sedulous attention is given in its pages to the collateral branches of the various noble families, and the names of many thousand individuals are introduced, which do not appear in other records of the titled classes. For its authority, correctness, and facility of arrangement, and the beauty of its typography and binding, the work is justly entitled to the place it occupies on the tables of Her Majesty and the Nobility.

LIST OF THE PRINCIPAL CONTENTS.

Historical View of the Peerage.
Parliamentary Roll of the House of Lords.
English, Scotch, and Irish Peers, in their orders of Precedence.
Alphabetical List of Peers of Great Britain and the United Kingdom, holding superior rank in the Scotch or Irish Peerage.
Alphabetical List of Scotch and Irish Peers, holding superior titles in the Peerage of Great Britain and the United Kingdom.
A Collective List of Peers, in their order of Precedence.
Table of Precedency among Men.
Table of Precedency among Women.
The Queen and the Royal Family.
Peers of the Blood Royal.
The Peerage, alphabetically arranged.
Families of such Extinct Peers as have left Widows or Issue.
Alphabetical List of the Surnames of all the Peers.

The Archbishops and Bishops of England, Ireland, and the Colonies.
The Baronetage, alphabetically arranged.
Alphabetical List of Surnames assumed by members of Noble Families.
Alphabetical List of the Second Titles of Peers, usually borne by their Eldest Sons.
Alphabetical Index to the Daughters of Dukes, Marquises, and Earls, who, having married Commoners, retain the title of Lady before their own Christian and their Husbands' Surnames.
Alphabetical Index to the Daughters of Viscounts and Barons, who having married Commoners, are styled Honourable Mrs.; and, in case of the husband being a Baronet or Knight, Honourable Lady.
Mottoes alphabetically arranged and translated.

"Lodge's Peerage must supersede all other works of the kind, for two reasons: first, it is on a better plan; and secondly, it is better executed. We can safely pronounce it to be the readiest, the most useful, and exactest of modern works on the subject."—*Spectator.*

"A work which corrects all errors of former works. It is a most useful publication."—*Times.*

"As perfect a Peerage as we are ever likely to see published."—*Herald.*

www.ingramcontent.com/pod-product-compliance
Lightning Source LLC
Chambersburg PA
CBHW020157170426
43199CB00010B/1081